ALL THAT NAMES US

ALL THAT NAMES US

KEITH WALKER

SADDLE ROAD PRESS

All That Names Us © 2024 Keith Walker

All rights reserved. No part of this book may be reproduced or transmitted in any form or by any means without written permission of the author.

Saddle Road Press
Ithaca, New York
saddleroadpress.com

Designed by Don Mitchell
Cover image by Keith Walker

ISBN 9798987954195
Library of Congress Control Number 2024933071

For Edite

Contents

I. A Bowl of Feathers

Belongings	13
Paper World	15
Call Home	17
Momma's Wing	18
My Life as a Subdivision	19
First Fish	21
Climbing Hatteras Light	22
Me and the King	23
The Feeler Gauge	25
Amends	28
The Weight of Wings	30
The Airmen's Home	33
Dishwasher's Lament	35
The News from Fort Fear	37
Finding Anne	39
For Dwight	42
All That Names Us	45
Sugarcane	47
Always April	49
The Baby Monitor	51
Momma's Last Cornbread	52
In Your Place	54
Overflight	57
A Bowl of Feathers	58

II. In Need of Rain

Girl at the Clinic	63
Hollis	66
The Woman Who Was a Hotel	68
Talking about Boats	74
Mike and Bob's Citgo	75
All-Night Sports Radio	77
Hill Street	78
Downtown Christmas	79
Post-Industrial	80
The Crosswalk at Main and North	81
The Smell of Rain on Asphalt	83
Crow	84
The Steps	85
In Need of Rain	86
Down by the River	91
East River, New York City	92
If I Could Paint Like Hopper	94
Rwanda—Day of Remembrance	95
"Battlefield in Northern France Strewn with German Dead"	96
Counting in the Trenches	98
Photographs of a Street in Lodz	99
Dreams of Time in Hell's Kitchen	101
One Sunday	103

III. Reduced to Prayer

Nothing Personal	107
Will You	109
Call to Prayer	110
Nothing Between	111
The Bruised Field	112
Night Drive	113
Down Water Street	114

THE LISTENING RIVER	115
WHAT THE RABBIT SAW	116
A PHOTOGRAPH IN THE LEXINGTON HOTEL	117
THE COVID HOURS	118
ADJUSTING TO THE LIGHT	122
HOME REMEDY FOR WRITER'S BLOCK	123
SOUNDINGS	124
WOOD ISLAND LIGHT	126
VESPER LAMP	127
FOR GOD SO LOVED	128
PRAYER OF UNNAMING	130
THE ACHE	132
GIVE IT TO THE FLAME	134
ACKNOWLEDGMENTS	137
ABOUT THE AUTHOR	139

I. A Bowl of Feathers

Belongings

This little green man with a boy's face
kneels on my shelf shouldering a bazooka.
Turning the soldier in my hand
I feel the spine of the mold,
scrapes from rocks in sandbox wars
and a slash in his thigh.
I forgot. I did that.

A gift from the boy next door
when I was three or four and we lived
in the asbestos-shingled apartments
in Altavista, Virginia—oil heater
in the narrow kitchen, railroad tracks
sunk into the red bank behind us.

I tripped on a tie and sliced my knee—
first lesson in blood—taste
of brine and rust. I still have the scar
and the name of the boy next door.

Benny drank RC Cola for breakfast
and had brown teeth. His daddy's nails
were black and he smelled like gasoline.
Some nights he whipped him good
when he got home from work.

My parents didn't like me going there.
My father belonged to the furniture plant
and stayed past dark working for something
he needed more than a raise or a son.
He came home empty to sit and stare.

My mother belonged
between the stove and sink
and behind the bedroom door
where she went to cry in the afternoon.

And I belonged to them and they loved me
so much it hurt. I learned to watch my mouth
and enjoy the company of toys.

I didn't like to share so they made me
put my tin ambulance in a bin
for the poor, after all it was dented and worn.
But I cried and wanted it back. I needed it
for unseen emergencies, like

the downed wires of their dreams
that filled our small rooms and shocked
when I pulled away
or came too close

my face lit by the arc
of a hand on fire.

Paper World

The shortest crayon
was always black.
Even though the ground
was waxy green,
the sky a thick
banner of blue—
and between them,
the world.

Chocolate trees
with arms and hands
each had a black hole
in the trunk—
how did we know so young
about empty places
the lemon sun's spokes
couldn't reach?

The stick family
and their crooked house
with its leaning chimney
always spiraling
a rope of smoke
floated above the ground
not yet subject
to laws of perspective
or the burdens of gravity.

Houses were faces,
hiding secrets
behind wide staring eyes.

In the colorless
in-between everything
needed thick black borders
to keep from disappearing
into the white void.

So we bore down
with our small black crayon
to hold it together.

Call Home

Momma would whistle
two notes of a sparrow
to call me home.

Now the sparrows
are only sparrows.
I wish a call

would interrupt my play. I'd clamber up
the back steps

through the unhooked
screen door
to supper

steaming on the stove.

Momma's Wing

when I dropped my fork
Momma would gasp—a fish
swallowing its young—

her hand fluttering
to the niche above her breast bone
like a startled bird

a wing sheltering
its secret nestling
from a hungry eye

the taste of fear
in my mother's milk
darkened my blood

My Life as a Subdivision

These streets, named for trees
that once shaded our hills, led nowhere
but where we lived—

fathers under cars,
mothers over stoves,
children learning to be them.

At our best we laughed
on Sunday nights
over TV trays.

Our house, now empty—
where I played army,
undressed my sister's dolls,

and hid my dirty drawings
in the trunks of model cars.
Out back, the cherry tree

where I pointed my sling shot
into a swarm of hungry grackles
to be my mother's hero.

She cursed them for eating
her cherries. I was gutted
when one fluttered awkwardly

over the roof, collapsing
in a heap of oily feathers.
Then she cursed me.

The day we moved out
left a hollow in me
like the dents in the floor.

I looked back at my window
staring out over the porch
where I'd lie after dusk,

feeling the sun held in its bricks.

First Fish

A flat muscle
big as my father's hand

and scaled with dimes
convulses from a thread

slapping blindly
beating like a rubber

mallet against the hull.
Leaded by its weight

out of water
it slips into the bilge

gills straining red
in our merciless air.

Climbing Hatteras Light

I climbed the light
at Cape Hatteras
with my father
while my mother
kept my sister for herself
in the foamy hem of the sea.

We funneled up
the spiraling iron stairs
and gazed into the geometries
of the glass hive of its eye.

On the lantern room parapet
a keen wind carries the scent
of the salted sky.

Nine landings above the shoals,
and my mother's realm
of worry, I forget to be afraid,
leaning out against the railing—
thrilling to the curve of the earth.

Me and the King

The first time I sang
was with you—
Hound Dog—on the gray Philco
in the kitchen of the Vetville
barracks at NC State.

And I strutted with you
in front of the grainy
TV that sat on legs
in our little apartment
in the Virginia foothills.

Your slick black hair
shined like my daddy's
and all the other men
who carried combs
and worked on their own cars.

But I grew up and shook
you off for the cool
of the Mersey boys.
I begged to grow my hair
and sang with them instead.

You embarrassed me
with your drive-in movies
your Hollywood tan
the silly staged dances
and pathetic romances.

I even laughed at you—
sweating in your tight jumpsuit
your upper lip frozen
your rawboned edge
tamed by Vegas,

dulled by pills—tossing
your wet handkerchiefs
to rows of bee-hived
martini-eyed women
my mother's age.

And when my neighbor
asked me to go see you
in Columbia six months
before you died, no,
just too redneck for me.

Now, looking out from black
velvet effigies in our bars
and trailers, and the back
room of my memory,
you weep for our broken
white-trash hearts.

The Feeler Gauge

My first homesick trip from college
you were disgusted by my hair—
a pile of shit thrown
against a barn door
and the tweed cap—
did you beat up a drunk
to steal that?
and my first semester's wisdom
earned a *goddamn, boy*
you think your shit
smells like a camelia?
as you smirked
and shook your head.

Later you declared a truce
as you always did
and asked me to help
while you tuned
the old blue Dodge.

I mostly held the light
while your hands, trained
on Hellcats in the Navy,
operated in the oily works
of internal combustion.

I handed you the sheaf
of thin metal blades
you used to gauge gaps.
You wanted me to feel
the hint of friction
in properly set points and plugs.

We washed up with borax
that left my hands stinging raw.

The muscle in the bend
of your elbow from your job
at the mattress factory
bulged like an egg
and the thick ropes across
the shoulders I squeezed
in our close moments
were still taut when I woke
in the chair beside your bed
to find you gone.

The spring I turned nine
and hemorrhaged
from a botched tonsillectomy
by **Dr. Kinser**—*better drunk
than anybody else sober*—
you promised me a bat and glove
and even took time
between work and golf
to practice with me
an hour before tryouts—
pleased to see your second baseman's
quickness in my hands
when I fielded your grounders,
disappointed to see the dynasty end
when I didn't make the cut.

On green evenings I watched
the ash between your fingers fall
in the damp grass and followed
the coiling white smoke.

Night filled the gulf
between us as the beer
turned warm but you still
got a reluctant laugh out of me
with a stale joke
in your hare-lip voice.

A window hanging in the dark
framed my mother
bent over the sink.

I wonder did you feel the gap
and know you'd waited too late,
left me too long
in my mother's shelter
reading away the afternoons,
learning the secret language
of each other's silence.

Amends

for Uncle "Cotton," Charles Aubrey Walker

So blond they called you Cotton
solid boy standing proud
on a mountain porch.

Eagle scout, big league
prospect, you saw action from
your blister turret

on Pacific nights,
flare-lit faces in landing craft
taking your tracers.

Hard-fisted you cleaned out
barracks full of Marines.
Daddy said their rings

made those little scars.
You hit the bottle harder
when peace dumped you home

cooking short orders
in cheap diners until you
got kicked out for good.

Your sons fought each other
until the walls bled. Neither lived
to heal from your wounds.

On your half-melted Zenith
we watched the big games
through a Pall Mall haze.

You knew every move,
a natural who still walked
with cocky grace.

Fourteen years sober
those chips worth more to you than
trophies and medals.

When they cut out your
voice you still picked up when I
called and rang a bell.

In your hospital bag
a Timex, a t-shirt, and two notes—
oxygen and pain

and the only card I sent
a canoe beached on the shore
of a wide river.

I didn't make it
in time to see you in the VA.
At the funeral home

a few tough young men
wept beside your coffin
and remained anonymous.

The Weight of Wings
for Uncle "Jiggs", Lt. Col. E.G. Walker (Ret.)

From a deep holler
in the shadow of the Blue Ridge
through white oak buds
you followed the sound
of beating air to the glint
of the mail plane's wings
and dreamed of climbing
above the mountain walls
from the aerie of your bedroom
where stick and paper birds
stirred from a low ceiling.

From the field at Horsham Saint Faith
aboard a mint B-24
you soared the Channel
and brushed the tidy farms
with a faint shadow
from seven miles high
until the cities lined up
in the crosshairs
of your Norden bombsight.
You lay face-down against
its thin riveted skin
watching the seeds
you sowed erupt silently
in blossoms of fire
followed by the soft
gloved knocks of detonation
that trailed in your wake
until the whistling flak
broke your wings and dropped you
into the North Sea.

As a boy in love with what
I thought was war
I asked you for the stories
of night raids, Messerschmitts,
the Stalag, your Flying Cross
and was left puzzled
by the dark silence
beneath grudging answers—
the crew that didn't make it
convoy lights winding
through Korean mountains
lit with napalm
long hauling atom bombs
over cold war skies
taking close ups
of burning jungles—
the weight of your wings.

You shunned the gray desk
to stay in the air
and flew Generals
rather than become one.
But your time was up
and you struggled on the ground
selling life insurance
playing golf to shoot your age
and taking night flights
fueled on highballs
until you entered the home
where airmen fall to earth
and even sea-level air
breathes too lean.

But you drove yourself
to see my mother
then your brother die
and called yourself a coward
with no stomach for guns
not even in movies
and you turned down
your proud daughter's wish
to honor you with a trip
to the War Memorial.

I've seen
enough death.

The Airmen's Home

The sky was on fire
singing with steel
when you were nineteen
plowing in on fresh wings.

Hands that feathered
thundering craft
faster than sound
struggle with a spoon
for the chocolate ice cream
I've smuggled in
remembering you craved it
when you were freed
from Stalag Luft III.

I am sometimes me
sometimes your brother
and you are sometimes you
grasping to get your bearings
on a faulty compass.

My boyhood hero
you took me to the flight line
and sat me in the cockpit
of your fighter plane.

I built plastic models
and dreamed of combat
until napalm and carpet
bombing burned them away.

How did your heart
survive three wars
without armor
to hold your tiny
old dog like a china cup
and feed her by hand
to sit with me
that endless week
watching my father die
to hold my hand
and cry with me
when I leave you
saluting with your heart.

Dishwasher's Lament

There was a moment
the summer I turned seventeen
washing dishes
in Myrtle Beach,
when I staggered
up Kings Highway
home to the cheap motel
where I never got lucky
with the college girls
who wanted their boys
fast and bad, not lost
and unschooled in the dance
of mutual use.
They guarded my innocence
with unwanted kindness.

There was a moment
in the sand with the moon
shattering on the arched
backs of waves, endlessly
caving on themselves

when skin
no longer marked
my boundaries
and the sea reclaimed me
until nothing was left
of not belonging

as I lay
between waves
between breaths
between stars

on the world's belly
in animal quiet.

The News from Fort Fear

A face on the news, one
only a mother could love,
sits in his chicken coop
fortress hung with swastikas
and rebel flags—
Sieg Heiling all to Hell
in the foothill accent
of my Tennessee childhood.

Those beautiful hills
and cruel boys.

)(

I walked home from school past Jimmy Snyder's
squat, peeling house, rusting cars in the yard
stuck in the overgrowth down by Turkey Creek.
Jimmy was two heads and two years taller
than everybody else. He slicked his hair back like his daddy,
who glared up from under a raised hood with narrow black eyes.
Jimmy stood up in Mrs Rowell's sixth grade class and told
Danny Susong to give him a pencil. Danny didn't.
His fist exploded with a flesh and bone sound
I'd never heard. We cowered and Danny tried to cry
but couldn't catch his breath, the red welt rising on his cheek.

)(

Maybe these men are all that's left
of boys ground down
into the red clay
until they're all scars
and no tears.

※

In his too-tall shiny jack boots
he stops strutting and returns
to his lawn chair,
babying his gun in his lap,
daring us to find
the pissing child behind
his mask of evil.

Finding Anne

I searched for you today
and found your black and white
class picture but not your red hair.

I've been wondering for years
and feared the worst.

We were both fifteen
but I was a lifetime behind you
our sophomore fall.
Friends said a red-haired girl
was following me through the halls.

So I turned and saw you—
part Hippie in tie-dye
part party girl in short skirt
and high-heel clogs.

Everyone had a story
about how good you were—
in the back seat
and in your small house
across the tracks
where rich and cool and beaten
boys all had their turn.

Did you see in my shy
unschooled awkwardness
what someone took from you?

I let myself become
your uncomfortable boyfriend
embarrassed, ashamed.

I was your somebody to love,
the way a young girl loves a boy
with cards and stuffed animals.

I hid them
from mocking friends
and my worried mother
and never responded in kind.

You went to church to prove
you'd changed but I was too weak,
too young not to be swayed
by all the ugly jokes
and when my mother
had our family doctor,
who knew you well, tell me
to get this monkey off my back,
that feeling sorry wasn't love,
I turned away.

I heard you had my picture
blown up into a poster
and still kept it on your wall.
You fled the state
when a deal went bad.

I searched for you today
but only found
it ended in San Diego
when I was in social work school.

Even my grief is thirty years late.

I joined Find a Grave,
added the "e" to your name
and left a card
with pixel roses.

No obituary, no red hair,
only dates on a bronze plaque
resting in dry Sumter dirt
touched by a stray weed.

For Dwight

You taught English at the old white school,
one of the first black teachers,
that jagged year of desegregation
and small riots. Our separate worlds
rarely touched outside the classroom.

Uncomfortable with your height,
you stooped through the halls—
looking down, somewhere else.

I was drawn to your silence,
deeper than shyness—
you seemed to have found
the way out of this life
between the swamps
and baked fields of Sumter
where I no longer belonged.

⚹

You let me visit.
The house you'd built,
a low brick bunker
with no front door,
windows covered
by a wall of breeze blocks.
Your sculpted faces
waivered in candlelight,
their eyes piercing, shamanic.

⚹

I'd snagged my hand
working at the furniture factory
my first summer in college,
and you needled the splinter out
with your sculpting tool,
laughing when I looked away,
my hand resting in yours.

When I had no more words
for the ache, your records
of Ella, Billie, Peggy, Sarah—
said it all
in indigo.

⚹

One night I stayed until two
and quietly opened the front door
of my parents' house
to my father's seething face
and my mother's distress—
*What the hell were you doing so late
on that side of town!
I was ready to call the police
to find out if you were dead!*
I had no way to translate
how alive I was.

⚹

Home from college at Christmas
in K-Mart, a few lanes over,
I saw you and looked away,
glimpsing you turning heavily
from my avoidance.

᙮

A few years later, at the end
of a call, my mother said—
that teacher you used to visit
out by the highway,
I saw in the paper, his house
caught on fire. He went back inside
to save some of his art
but didn't make it out.

᙮

Half a life and more has gone by,
then last night you showed up
in the blankness of sleep.
I want to say I'm sorry.

I have no place to hide
from your sly half-smile

amused it's taken me this long
to finally know
why.

All That Names Us

Pulling the worn thread clicks
the bare bulb and brings to light
the cardboard boxes beginning
to bulge like aging cheeses—

boxes layered with notebooks
filled with thoughts—
thoughts too important
to forget. Files of notes
from social work internships—
the scrawled names of children
and their drawings
looking out at me for help—
my help that came and left.

My paper on Dante for my mentor,
the Ulysses Canto, the hubris
of my fountain-penned insights
washed to pale blue blossoms
from a leak in the roof. Digging
lower to my drawings

from childhood—a colossal lighthouse,
a watercolor of a melting blue house
guarded by a dripping stop sign,
a sky knotted with fighter planes,

their guns firing dashes
across the page, sending a Messerschmitt
down in flames, a copied still-life
in pastels that actually showed promise,

a car, so detailed I used my father's
drafting tools—unfinished,
and a bubbling psychedelic dreamscape
imitating Cream album covers—
pretending to be from trips
I was too afraid to take.

Here's my wallet from junior high
that once held a sticker of a rebel flag,
replaced by a peace sign and the label
from a bottle of bourbon.

And a box of my mother's china—
the good china kept perfect
by non-use just the way
she taught me,
delicate lavender tendrils
untouched by light.

Sugarcane

I think daddy did love momma.
That night looking for her brother's place
past the cotton mill this side of Cheraw
with rain smacking welts on the windshield,
she said she saw sugarcane.
She said *sugarcane* like it was

somebody's name, like somebody
she knew from down home.
I looked back at the row of tall shoots
under a string of dripping lights
leaned against the wall
of a cinderblock service station

and before she could ask
he turned the Mercury around
and pulled into the lot
with wet gravel crunching
and popping under our tires.
He trotted back, drenched,

and shoved the sharp leaves
over the seat, shedding cold
rain on my sister and me.
He clicked open his pocket knife
and carved the tough stalk
down to pale seeping pulp.

We sat while heavy drops
pocked the car and crawled
down the fogging windows.
She bit into raw sweetness
and went down somewhere alone.

Was it that wide bleached field
surrounded by bony pines
in the flaking photograph—
the one with your mother smiling
in a white Sunday dress
and you, curling from the hard sun
into the crook of her arm?

Always April

April always brings
your taxi to the Tar River—
the merry-go-round still

boarded up in Sunset Park
that wet dim morning—
where you left your bag

and your small suitcase,
the one you always traveled
with to visit

and your beige raincoat
neatly folded and your cat-eye glasses
where you walked into the water

where the river pulls
the shadows of pines
down to Pamlico Sound,

the reaching limbs
holding you close to shore,
yawing in the shallows.

The neighbors said you went
to work in shoes that didn't match
and brought home clothes

for the grandchildren that weren't paid for,
from Belks, where you'd walked the floors
ever since Papa died

and came home to bake me
a lemon meringue pie from scratch
and left it waiting on the water heater.

Your weekly white postcards
stopped, Momma burned supper
and ran to her room to cry.

I always forget the day.
But year after year
I know when it comes—

buried shells of grief,
still holding their charge after
fifty years of silence.

You freed yourself
and us from watching
you unravel.

You rocked me to sleep
with a lullaby
in the chair my sister has:

Go tell Aunt Rhody
the old gray goose is dead
she died in the millpond…

Your bible open
to *he leadeth me*
beside the still waters

on the coffee table
with the scent of magnolias
floating in a bowl.

The Baby Monitor

We bought a baby monitor to hear
my mother in her rented bed
in the living room.

Small red lights followed each breath.
Her sips of air became shallow,
the lights went dark.

We sat under the pines
my dad grew from seedlings,
the speaker falling mute,

except for the sparrows
outside her window
bathing in the dust.

Momma's Last Cornbread

I learned to crank you out of the hospital bed
in the living room into a wheelchair.

We passed by the guest room, piled with recipes
and décor ideas from *Southern Living*

and diets for weight loss, blood pressure, diabetes
next to the closet packed with clothes you couldn't wear.

Then, to your bedroom, certain it would make you cry.
You stared—at the dresser, your jewelry and perfumes,

curling photographs and trinkets from us—
like it was someone else's life.

We eased down the new ramp to see the yard—
the dogwoods and azaleas planted under longleaf pines.

After brushing and smelling the sprawling Lady Banks rose
from your mother's yard, by the carport, you said

I don't think I need to see this again.

You shocked me by asking me to take away
the TV you'd eaten and slept in front of.

For twenty years, you and Daddy drove home for lunch
to watch soap operas together over boiled ham sandwiches.

You listened to old 78s that hissed and popped. Your feet danced
out from under the sheets swaying with Jimmy Dorsey—

Tangerine, she is all they claim
With her eyes of night and lips as bright as flame

Your last night, you watched my sister and me keeping watch
over you, told each of us in a cute girlish voice:

Now you go to sleep,
now you go to sleep.

Dr. Givens stopped by in the morning to say goodbye.
You joked about him not finding your pulse.

When it was just us, you said, *I think I'll let you*
open the curtains.

I want to see the children
across the street.

I don't think I've ever
seen it so bright.

You can close them now.

Thinning into light, you asked for cornmeal,
your hands mixing it with flour in the air.

If I could just put my feet on the floor
and get out of this bed.

You pushed away the sheet
and pulled at your gown.

We swear you passed through us
on your way out.

In Your Place
for Marty

The small plane follows the river,
greening walls on either side,
as we descend into Asheville.

I'm flying in to walk your daughter
down the aisle on Saturday.
The houses spread further

up the mountains. I turn up
Sweeten Creek, taking
the way you used to drive me

where the blue mountains
roll towards dusk, down Mills Gap
past the Goodwill and the Shell

at the bottom of the hill,
pulling up under the poplars
that hide your house in shade.

Four years gone.
Your wife, my sister, still wears
shadows under her eyes.

When she and I run out of words,
I try to hear your voice,
the hard r's of Buffalo

smoothed by thirty years down south.
I allow myself to sit in your place—
that overstuffed chair, too big for you,

to look at the world you watched ending.
The blue chair, where you'd add a flourish
of air guitar to a new song

you were eager to play for me.
I still have all the personalized
mixtapes you made, filled

with your love of music, and now
I know, with love for me.
We sat here drinking perfectly

poured Black and Tans—
you, excited about your classes
and students and playing bass

in a band. And I see you
too, holed up in this chair,
hidden behind lesson plans,

earphones, beer cans,
unreachable for days on end.
Your boyish frame left only socks

and a blue striped shirt that I can wear.
That shirt must have swallowed you.
Swallowed you like those so-called

small cells did in seven weeks
years after you gave up
the solace of smoke.

I keep the card you sent—
For My Brother—
grieving the time we'd never spend.

I should visit you in the garth
near St. Francis and his concrete birds
but you are everywhere but there.

Overflight

Like a ghost plane—
a faint cross of chalk
at the edge of space—
you appear out of nowhere.

Is your long fall forgotten
the way climbers,
at home in the air,
lose touch with the ground?

Do you look down and follow
the Swannanoa to Asheville—
worn into the warp and weft
of the Blue Ridge

to find your old house
in the cul de sac
near the Weston Branch
on the slope of Brown Mountain?

Do sparks of your life
remain, or have you lost
all need for them, like fish
never rising for air?

Drifting above the world,
wheels frozen in their wells,
last light catches
the arc of your trail.

A Bowl of Feathers

Your body let you go
and left me here
to rummage through boxes
of yellowing paperback westerns,
scratched 78s of big bands and crooners
and racks of gaudy golf shirts
from the dollar store.

There's no resurrecting you
from this mess, though I try—
putting feathers in a bowl
and waiting for them to sing.

Where to look for you—
between the stars or feeling
my way along these shapeless
walls inside me,
until I find the room
where grief accumulates—

a storage room, like your closets
piled with old shoes, your shed
littered with half-finished projects.

I can't find you
in the things you touched—

not in your hand tools, dark with use,
mechanical drawing instruments,
corroded by time,
your blue plaid shirts
I can no longer wear—

your relics—now enshrined
in my garage, on my bookshelves,
in the back of my closet.

⁂

I'm like a worshiper
in that native cult
of the South Pacific who still
makes altars to the gods that floated
down from the sky, then flew away
when the war was over,

building planes from twigs and straw
and a bamboo control tower

calling calling calling

through a tin can
for the giant silk blossoms
of cargo from heaven.

Like him, I burn torches
by the abandoned runway

waiting to be crossed
by the shadow of your wings.

II. In Need of Rain

Girl at the Clinic

You were a child of the state
from the Angel Guardian Home.
They took you when you stole
your foster mother's ring.
I was a second-year social work intern
working in Flatlands, Brooklyn.

I watched you roll yellow Play-Doh into gold
and make believe you had a million dollars
to buy your mother anything she wanted,
your real mother, on Staten Island,
who was gone on powder.

You drew her building over and over,
then painted it with all the colors
until there was only a layer of mud
that dried and cracked open.

You drew your face with a big circle,
a saucer open to the sky,
sifting heaven's static
for a tiny message
with your name on it.

You drew me a picture
of a girl with a gift.
You were a gift to me.

You wanted to type a story
but gave up on words,
hammering the keys
until they jammed.

On my last day, I worried
how to say good-bye. Outside,
you found a broken flower
and planted it
in a hill of dirt.

Your small arms clung
to me as if I were the mother
you couldn't hold.

        ⚘

You would be a woman now,
somewhere in New York.

I search the misspelling
of the African country
your mother named you for
and instantly your trail appears
from Brownsville to Bed-Stuy
and back to Staten Island.

And a link I can't help opening—
"Fatal Shooting of Staten Island Teen."

Relief. You're only the relative
in the Eyewitness News clip
where police mark evidence
on a taped-off street in the projects.

You stand in front of candles
and posters on a basketball court
and look straight into the lens

your face and shoulders
lean and strong,
She was on her way
she never hurt nobody
it's very sad,
long done with tears.

Hollis

I knew him from the diner
red faced in a white apron
sweating all winter long.

Short, stocky, and strong—
military sidewalls
wide pale-blue eyes.

He jogged bussing tables
shuffling plates into tilting
stacks like Popeye, and dealt

flatware and mugs smack
down on the wet counter.
If he caught me looking

he bet *you never seen
nobody this fast.*
He debated the dishwasher

*who'd you rather fight
a great white shark or a saber tooth tiger.*
After they went out of business,

replaced by a bar and gallery,
I would see him pacing
all over the city. He'd nod

but never slowed down.
He thinned and stopped looking up.
One July in the square

he stepped out of the crowd,
sun beaten and unclean.
He met my eyes and whispered

remember me, can you spare
a dollar—glassy-eyed
electric as a prophet.

The Woman Who Was a Hotel

The Lobby

I knew a woman who was a hotel.
At first, she was simply *Mrs. White*.
She came to see me
because she was losing time—

hours and days that vanished—
and her life before her children
was a black hole. One day she dropped
a bottle of beer and started to shrink.

The Office

For weeks, you tested me
bringing me food
and plants for my office
to keep me at a distance.

One day you curled
into the corner of the sofa
cuddling a bear, and spoke
in a voice I'd never heard.

In the Hallway

The hotel walls are thin
and voices begin leaking through
breaking the rules: be quiet
and never leave your room.

The rooms are bolted, but the smell
of Old Spice or Black Velvet tobacco,

or the family photo over your sister's couch
can trip the locks and open doors

on bewildered girls who are never
a day older than the day they checked in—
each holding a shard of mirror
and hiding an open wound.

Room 1

This girl is named *Little*
with "hair colored hair"
she wants to cut it off
because *he* clenches it.

Little trembles and whispers
my stomach hurts, I always feel sick…
If I tell, he'll kill me.
He really will—

he drowned my cat.
This is what God gave little girls
to their fathers for.
A different voice cuts her off.

Shut up! This one's cold
and tough and in control.
Her edgy laugh and glare
both an invitation and a dare.

Room 2

Belle runs the front desk.
She will be my guide.
Over weeks and years, she unlocks
doors. Inside every room

a man and a girl.
Belle knows the hotel
and *Belle* knows men
and how to manage them both.

She can wither with a look,
a fuck, or a broken bottle.

She will do anything to survive.
Anything.

I don't cry. I can't cry. I don't feel.
I won't let anyone hurt me.
And a man only gets me
when I make him, Darlin'.

Room 3

Ragdoll. She's five years old.
He does things to her,
while men, who drink and stink
of the paper mill, watch.

Room 4

Bessie Mae is eight when he
starts to make her hurt.
She screams but her mother
never comes. She never screams again.

Room 5

Sally is thirteen. She visits
with her aunt and uncle
who seem so normal,
but *he* likes her that way, too.

Sally is surrounded by men
in white talking about her
like she's not there, shocked
to find a dead baby inside.

Sally used to hope it would stop—
other kids' fathers didn't do that.
But one hot day in a blueberry field
he kisses her until it feels good.

He tells her she loves it and wants it,
she's just like him, and she says *yes*.
She tries to drown herself in the river
where he made her wash off.

Room 6

And *Belle of the Ball* is born.
Don't be such a goddamned baby!
Yeah, it's awful, but sex is sex.
You don't let it kill you!

Belle is afraid of *Suicidal Sally*—
she feels, she cries, she's wracked
with shame. She hates water, it burns her body.
She's afraid of men, including me.

If she cashes in, she'll take us all
with her. I keep an eye out for her.
Mrs. White can't keep her off the pills.
It's all up to me, Darlin'.

Room 7

I'm *Nobody. I don't think.*
I can't think. I'm invisible.

I can go anywhere I want.
I can make you go away.

Room 8

Kathy, the sweet and innocent teen,
comes out for the nice boys—
she's the one with no past. But
she lets them come too close.

Belle sneers at *Kathy*—going soft
over insipid boyfriends while she's
taking punches from Rhode Island
mobsters to pay the rent.

Room 9

Anne knows they're not real
and maybe she isn't real.
She wants to know what is real
and stop pretending.

She walks in the woods
and finds beauty in the trees
and peace in the clouds. *I'm not
important. I may never come back.*

The Suite

One by one, *Belle* lets Mrs. White
meet them all, when she thinks
she's strong enough to take it.

One day she asks, *If I go away,
will you miss me, Darlin'?*
Yes, I will. I do.

Even though you and I both
know Mrs. White needs the keys now.
She paid the bill.

She knows *He can't kill me.*
He can't hurt me anymore.
It's not happening to me now.
I can see myself, all of me.

⋈

After three years, you stopped,
and disappeared.

Sometimes, I'd pick up the phone
to silence. Then, a quavering whisper

lets me know you're there,
needing my voice to bring you back.

After a long lapse, I go searching for you
and read you died last spring.

The obituary shows you at your cabin,
smiling with your whole face.

I imagine a field where the walls once stood,
the foundations, now overgrown—

saplings filling in the ruins
finding the sky.

Talking about Boats

Two men in a truck
at the mouth of the river
talk about boats.

Next week one will lie
in a cold white room waiting
to be opened up.

One man sweeps his hand
mimicking the gentle slope
of a Jonesport hull.

One half-listening
stares through the windshield out past
the waves on the jetty.

Two cormorants scissor
above them, never parting
never quite touching.

Mike and Bob's Citgo

and liquor store—an island
of cold light in the still dark
hours on Elm Street

where a gaggle of men
graying under Red Sox, Bruins,
and *Don't Tread on Me* hats

gathers by the counter
in well-worn plaid and camo
drinking coffee. Fed up

with their Brady-less
Patriots who gave it away
last night, leaving them

to face another shift—grinding
turbines at Pratt & Whitney
for fighter planes

or boring barrels for machine
guns at Saco Defense—
without a champion.

Alright, one last pat
down for smokes
and a refill for the ride.

Stiffly pulling themselves up
into idling trucks—stickered
with rage and pride—

they rumble off, refueled
on what in these parts
passes for love.

All-Night Sports Radio

Men alone, calling in
deep in the night,
slurring at the host—
who's smoked or yelled
himself to a rasp—
between endless ads
for online betting
and divorce lawyers.

Some spar with statistics,
breaking down
every player's game
and every team's chances
with a gambler's eye
for an edge
to cover the spread
and beat the odds.

Some cling to their tribe
with devotion like blood.
Perhaps to the team
of their fathers.
Perhaps to the sport they played
to please their fathers.
Perhaps to keep hold
of the one thing they shared.

I'm still up
with them, listening—
putting off the night
without sleep, without dreams
of an absent father.

Hill Street

Across the river
above tattoo parlors
and storefront missions,
on a spent Sunday
I walk after dark.

Bare fluorescent tubes
hung from dropped ceilings
fill the rooms, walled with fake
paneling and curled photographs,
with bluish light.

Down a side street
men's beer voices carom
between narrow mill houses.
Their sons make war with sticks
under a salmon streetlight—

practicing, the way we did,
how to fall and die.

Downtown Christmas

Three wandering men
bearing their worlds
in backpacks
rest in the bus shelter
sharing a smoke
and cold comfort
from a brown paper bag.

Arguing in loud rasps
of shoveled gravel—
voices blown but still
raging to be heard,
the morning after
silent night.

Post-Industrial

The Biddeford mill stack,
defunct and floodlit now, towers
over the Saco race
above brew pubs and boutiques

and weaving rooms redone
in industrial chic, where once
Acadian farm girls worked
machines and breathed the dust.

Their granddaughters slouch
on tenement steps in their pajamas,
sunken-faced, smoking, yelling
through the door at screaming children.

The Crosswalk at Main and North

Nine degrees at the red light—
her camo jacket too thin.
Raw gusts lashing pink hair
across her grimace—waiting
to cross Main at rush hour
with her rickety stroller
and child who drops his toy
and stiffens and flails.

With my heat blasting
and music cranked I can't
hear the scream
his face all mouth
as she barks and slaps
at the air while bending down
trying to get the toy
from the gutter, trying
to keep the stroller
from rolling into the street.

But there's no magic
to soothe him now.
She jolts off the curb,
yanks back
from the truck speeding
through the intersection,
forces her way across—
stroller wheels jittering
like a bad grocery cart.

Feeling my eyes, she stabs
with a look—something
between goddamn you
and somebody help me.

As the light changes
I turn down the volume
and meet her eyes
to give his cry and her eyes
someplace to go.

The Smell of Rain on Asphalt

Surfing the net leads
from Ötsi the Ice Man
to an autopsy video.
I couldn't not watch,
like Da Vinci enthralled
by the mysteries beneath the skin,
mapping our unlit terrain
with a scalpel eye.

I stare in horror and awe
as a woman turns to intricate meat—
her torso opened neatly
as a zippered jacket—
to reveal signs of an overdose
in her stomach
and child-bearing in her womb.

Perhaps our little season
in baffled flesh
is the work of dark light
drawing its face in the dust
for a glimpse of itself.

The light is all gone
from the blossom of white matter
where the smell of coffee and roses
and chalk and cigarettes
and rain on asphalt lived.

Crow

A hole in this painted world
Crow waits.
Crow leans and drops.
Crow casts a shadow
on cold flesh.
Crow steals the thread
from the seams of dreams.
Crow spreads its wings—
a deck of cards
all black.
Pick yours.

The Steps

I heard the footsteps
of the new tenant
on the outside stairs
of the house where the man
shot his family and himself.

In this world of bones
the steps of a man
holding a child
the steps of a man
holding a gun
share this single sound.

The heart has a shelf
for everything.

In Need of Rain

The news showed, as news does,
the house where you lived—
a house like any house—
close to where I grew up.

I've passed the place a hundred times,
crossing the swamp from Sumter
to Columbia, but never noticed it,
set back off the highway.

I was always looking the other way
past the stretch of barbed wire
for the air base gate, guarded
by the fighter planes on pedestals

I dreamed of flying into combat.

⚜

Your father and mother pulled
you from town to town, school
to school and swatted you
back and forth when they split.

You—the quiet one,
frail, invisible—the boy
nobody really knew,
who never made anybody proud.

On the news, your dad walked
from the house, where you'd littered

the back yard with brass casings—
shirtless, his barrel chest overgrown

with tattoos and glinting with piercings,
turning to glare into the lens.

⚜

When I was your age, we drove
through these fields after dark
and parked on sandy tractor roads
guzzling our beer before it got warm,

blaring *Midnight Rider,* breathing in
the smell of sun and pesticide
in the cotton fields, waiting for night's
cool to seep from scorched South Carolina dirt.

⚜

I know the low slab houses and bungalows
where your life happened.
And the weedy crossroad town
without a stoplight

where you dropped out
in your friend's trailer—sleeping
on the floor, marking time
with drugs and vodka coolers,

and nights on the dark web
where you found your tribe.

I've passed the place just across
the Congaree River, Shooter's
Choice, where you bought your Glock—
a black .45, a birthday

present from your father.
You posed squinting down
the barrel like I once did
with my six-shooter from Santa.

You stare over your blue aviators
in a sagging Gold's Gym tank top,
holding your little Rebel flag on a stick,
aiming right into the eye of your camera,

working on your smirk—
the last thing nine people will see.

)(

You sat in the room with them
for forty-five minutes of Bible study,
before finally deciding
to unleash your truth.

They invited you to stand and pray with them—
Y'all want something to pray about
I'll give you something to pray about.
I have to do this. You're raping our women

and taking over the country.
You left one of your five empty
magazines next to the open Bible
on the table above where the preacher

lay on the Mother Emanuel
basement floor.

⚔

When the FBI got you, you talked
like an embarrassed kid,
snickering, *my mom's gonna be
really upset when she finds out*—

your gun still on the back seat
with a carton of Sprite, a box
of hollow points and cold fries.
How many? I'm not sure.

*I shot as fast as I could before
they could run.
I think maybe five. Nine? Really?
I feel kinda bad it was nine,*

but I didn't shoot anybody in the face.
Your only discomfort
was being photographed.
You fluffed your bowl-cut hair

for your mug shot
like it was a yearbook picture.

⚔

Back home with my dying mother,
her nurse Ruby invites me to church.
Turning off the beach highway
onto the road to Florence—

all flat fields and rows of pulp pines
even as fence posts.
On a bare sandy rise—
Beulah African Methodist Episcopal.

I'm late and the only white face—
the usher asks warily, *can I help you?*
Ruby turns and takes me to her pew.
In prayer, they hold hands,

a young man reaches for mine.

)(

Driving back, the bleaching sun
burns from everywhere,
currents of heat blur the pines.
I dream the smell of rain

and wonder what coils and waits
to rise from this ruined ground.

Down by the River

We say it, we sing it,
we end up here when we have
too much time, not enough love.

The grassy bank, littered
with crushed cans that failed to fill,
and half-eaten gas station sandwiches,

matted in the shape of a man
who breathed through cigarettes
and tired of his plaid shirt—

and sat here like me,
listening for something lost
in the river's breath.

East River, New York City

Drawn down to water
from the avenues
through side streets
and tenements in shadows
heavy with frying oil and corn.

Visitors at the VA
leave in Sunday clothes
by the iron gates of the old asylum
where 30th Street dead ends
under the FDR
hammering with traffic
at weekend's end.

Gulls wind down like ash
and strafe a rusting scow.

A deep tanker glides
through the last reach of the sun—
like a factory worked loose
and drifting off unnoticed
by workmen on the stairways.

The lead river bends
and sucks along the hull.
Black stones rise
in the wake and drop
with a hollow knock.

A gust between towers
shivers the river
like a horse's flank.

A rawness like rock salt
burns in my chest
where something behind
the face of the world
presses to get in.

If I Could Paint Like Hopper

I would draw you into this room
in the long brick façade

of the old railroad offices
where the woman in a scarlet top

sits on the brown couch
and the man in the charcoal sweater

watches from the blue chair.
Her gaze fixed on the ivory

medallion rug as his eyes watch
the face of a frozen clock.

Shadows from the glass table lamp
smoke the powdery walls.

Through the tall window
the sky drains to a pale green.

The smoldering hills trail off
into indifferent immensity.

Rwanda—Day of Remembrance

today is the day
time runs the wrong way

and the river of pain
crawls back to the plains

to the dark gurgling spring
of an open wound

where for a hundred days
by machete, stick and stone

on dusty roads
on river banks

in the ash of a charred church

one woman one man,
one boy one baby one girl

died a million times

each one looking out
through our eyes
crying from our heart

why hast thou forsaken

"Battlefield in Northern France Strewn with German Dead"

After brunch I found them
in a leather box on the coffee table,
Stereographs of the Great War—
each one curled
like a sleeping hand.

Inside the wooden
mask November clouds
dim a field of stubble
sloping to the Marne.
Rows of dried stalks
seem to step away.
Bare earth
shows through,
scalp pale.

Heaps of wool
crowd between hedgerows,
as heedless of one another
as bathers on a strand
lost to the sea.

Shrouded under great coats,
lucky pfennigs and lockets
of hair, nest inside
sinking tunics.

A caped figure blurs
to a forked smudge
as his polished boots stride
past white buttocks
in a pile of rags.

The far trees hang
like oil smoke.

Counting in the Trenches

Miles of crouching hearts
flinch at the hissing sky,
but you don't hear
the one that cleans you
from your bones.

The shower of singing iron,
the gut punch of air,
the cries down the line
say this was not yours
the dark reloads.

You count your breaths
between flash and thunder.

Microphones planted
in no man's land
listening for movement
in the wire
and gauging the range
of enemy guns
captured the eleventh hour
of the eleventh day.

The full onslaught
of artillery fire
thinning to distinct
detonations.

Stunned silence.

The voice
of a bird.

Photographs of a Street in Lodz

1.

People crawl out of a cart, where the street dead ends
at a fresh brick wall and barbed wire.

2.

In vacant tenements with nothing to burn,
they wear all the clothes they have.

3.

Children play in a pile of cobblestones
pretending they are loaves of bread.

4.

Faces in the bakery smile out of habit
pulling matzos from the charred oven door.

5.

Tram riders glance up from papers
at milling forms, draped in blankets.

6.

Carrying their lives in sacks
thawing earth pulls at their shoes.

7.

Following their own pale shadows,
they march toward the trains.

8.

Night gathers in the pots
left behind.

Dreams of Time in Hell's Kitchen

I wake in a Hell's Kitchen hotel room
walled with mirrors to make it larger.
Seeing myself wherever I look
the walls move even closer.

High enough to dream through
Saturday morning on Ninth Avenue,
I'm left with a fading fragment—
the house I grew up in, reduced to fine ash.

Sifting, I catch the glint of brass gears
from my grandmother's mantel clock
and the ring that held its face.
The gong is missing that marked the hours.

⚜

After a nostalgic bagel, I climb
the granite stairs of the Metropolitan
and escape the din through a small entrance
into an unvisited gallery.

Shiva stands dancing in a glass cube
inside a ring marked with flames,
drumming the dream of time.
Between beats, stars ignite and burn away.

⚜

In the Garment District where I shortcut
to visit my old building in Murray Hill,
an ancient man in the navy pinstripe suit
he's shrunk inside of, shuffles
as the crowd swarms past.

He pauses. From under his fedora,
blending in with the soot coated façades,
he searches a darkened storefront,
beckoned by ghosts I cannot see.

One Sunday

We fall asleep easily
behind curtains soaked
through with moonlight.
Somewhere towards day
a tap begins to drip
in a white-tiled room
inside a dream,
and I wake, afraid.
We lie mirroring each other
our arms crossed
like mummies.
I slide my foot to rest
in the hollow of yours,
but you turn and bear
yourself up before the weight
of morning settles,
plodding on stiff joints
to coffee and the *Times*.
Draped across the back
of a chair, your blouse
fills with light.

)(

I don't honestly care
for hymns and choirs
but go to be beside you
when your voice
catches in a song
and your face fills up
and I hear the German girl
inside your flawless English.

Your heavy-lidded Dietrich
always gets to me
...*wie einst Lili Marleen.*
Your contralto hums
through my hand
in the small of your back.
You sense my eyes
and let slip
an embarrassed smile.
I shift away
so you don't see my dread
of the day when these
memories work through me
like slivers of porcelain.

III. Reduced to Prayer

Nothing Personal

We all liked Jesus a lot—
said the team's manager.
It was nothing personal,
but we need more pitching.
And I thought, Jesus
I liked you too—
especially that painting
on the Sunday School wall,
a lamb resting its face
in the cup of your palm.

My icons came
with bubble gum
the summer Maris hit 61,
and a sparrow hurled
itself against the sky
in our picture window.

A bean bag filled
with little bones, it left
an oily print of down and dust,
huddling into the grass
under the shade of the eaves,
where I saw the sky
in the beads of ink
that were its eyes.

I dressed his damp skull
with first aid cream
and sheltered him
under a cardboard box.
I said my bedtime prayer
and placed him in your hands.

Before I woke, my father
had already taken care
to hide the evidence—
you don't fix
errant sparrows.
You don't stop the earth
from shaking down cities
or stop grandmothers
when spring beckons them
to walk into the river.

When helixes in my coding
turned my prostate cells rabid,
like my father's, like his brother's,
you didn't fix those either.

I know
it's nothing personal.

Will You

Wherever you are,
I need more than your vast
emptiness today.

I used to mock those
paintings of you with a face
and hands just like ours.

Now I want to picture
you with eyes to see me
and hands to touch me.

If I surrender my house
of names and make you
a room, will you stay?

Call to Prayer

Lined up against the breeze,
gulls pivot like weathervanes
and hunker on the sand.

A man, a woman, and a girl
settle around the table on the spit
of rocks by the landing.

The woman faces the sea
in her fluttering hijab,
letting the gusts lift her arms.

The man holds a thread
sloping down from the sky
as if it were tied to a bird.

The girl rests her face,
encircled in white silk.
on the table beside her music.

Chants and pulsing drums
surge and fade in the wind
lacing the sky with longing.

Nothing Between

When I drifted down
into the bottomless heart,
I lost some of my treasures.

My little bear, darkened by small hands
and tears, who knew my secret name,
was left behind on the bus.

The name you answered to
disappeared from the phone book
along with your last known address.

My favorite picture of you
fell out of its frame—
not the one of your burning heart

gift-wrapped in thorns,
but you standing outside the door
holding a lantern, knocking.

I keep that empty frame
propped in my window and now
I find it, a perfect likeness.

The Bruised Field

Mown fields drape down
from the dark wreck of mountains.

The dust of old light gathers
on cold brick earth.

Music of dead stars
hums in my ancient hands.

My way home across
the frosted grass is marked

with the darkening bruises
of every step I take.

Under the rising wing of a galaxy,
a bare tree opens its veins.

Night Drive

Driving between sheer faces
cut through the granite waves

of the Alleghenies, bleeding black,
freezing to crystal in the weaving

headlights of the last car
in West Virginia. Finally, a pull off

where we relieve ourselves,
overlooking a comatose city

of mercury and sodium vapor bulbs
planted in neat rows—

a nursery of stars, drifting up
into the reach of night.

Down Water Street

Dimming fire hangs snared
in the outline of pines
and power lines.

The river draws the dark
from the hills and dulls
the world's edges.

Above the spillway,
silence enfolds my dread
of no longer being here.

Waiting in the dark,
my eyes begin to open
to the bowl of light

nesting within—forever spilling.
I will try to dance
until the music turns to light.

The Listening River

The river reveals its secret
in a breath I will not live
to hear the end of
as it chafes through
bedrock to the sea.

Another river listens
within this river
for the murmuring secrets
hidden inside the world,
where the shadow of the pine
and my shadow meet
on a worn granite ledge.

One river wears away stone
the other whispers away
my names,
and when my eyes open
in the dark,
it shimmers.

What the Rabbit Saw

Morning light glows through
the petal-thin rabbit's ears
as we meet in wet grass.

The rabbit holds me
in its round brown
jewel of an eye

that sees the predator
in my frontal stare
and the smile that cleans

flesh from bone,
no matter how much
I wish to calm

its frozen fear
its madly beating vein.
I need a rabbit's eye

wide and unblinking
to know the teeth
hiding in my heart.

A Photograph in the Lexington Hotel

A deserted city park
in black and white—
the rain has just stopped,
still dripping from the globes
perched on ornate cast iron posts
along a gleaming cobbled path
lined with empty benches
and leafless trees.

The photograph and piano-black
frame, large as a door
stood by the stairs that wind
up to the Deco mezzanine.

The hotel has been remodeled
in vinyl and chrome.

The photograph–
the colonnade of gaslights
the draped strands
of bulbs burning halos
through the mist–
gone.

My searches, even the rainy dark
of Brassaï and Cartier-Bresson,
come up with only a similar lamppost
on the banks of the Thames.

Nowhere, the path
leading beyond the frame
into that perfect
unwritten night.

The Covid Hours

i.

The City Hall clock hasn't moved
since March, hands stuck
like all of us, at a minute to midnight.

There are no cars on Main Street—
the bricks of old buildings
breathe in the dark.

Under the silent streets,
the earth turns and remembers
life without us.

A long train calls out
and from across the river
a ghost train answers back.

ii.

The first petals open
with a scent of irony
in the locked-down spring.

A single leaf
hangs in the bare elm,
a lost wing beating the air.

All our wings are beating
to where we hope love has gone,
but can't escape this gravity.

Birds sing, sweetly oblivious.
I sing the only hymn I have:
Goddamn everything not breaking with grief.

iii.

Numbed by numbers,
refrigerated trailers, shadow-eyed nurses
I'm drawn to the Atlantic at Camp Ellis.

I want to walk out into the waves
and emerge with my heart thawed
and dripping with mercy

to follow the murmuration
of all the hurt of the world to where
it forms the heart of God.

iv.

I can find no way
to enter the world
except through this hole in my heart.

Most days, the yearning
is the only sign I have
of what I long for.

Piece by piece, this has
taken me apart and now
I'm reduced to prayer.

v.

Hollowed out,
something like a prayer
echoes endlessly.

Parking lot sparrows
repeat my heart's
one-note cry.

vi.

I realize too late
I have loved at a distance.
Now I must turn toward the heart

or toward water
where the shallow dish of moonlight
lies shattered on the river's back

and bleeds toward you
its shards healing
in the heart's dark eye.

vii.

For half an evening, Django
brings back the magic of summer nights,
and hymns of Bill Evans offer solace.

One last glance at the moon
floating unfazed above the pleading world
as I turn out the lights behind me.

In every room is
something to make me smile
and something to make me cry.

I hear time following me
in the hollow rasp
of my slippers on the floor.

viii.

Feeling my way to bed,
inhabited still with this presence
we bear, not quite our own.

I wait in this niche
in the dark's unbroken wall,
for the light I can no longer see.

Adjusting to the Light
for Pat

You lived from a place
that will be lost to us
until we become fluent

in the sign language
of love that spoke
through your simplest gestures,

reaching out from your pain
with hand-written notes
to comfort us.

We can't adjust our eyes,
to this dark.
So, breath by breath, we wait.

Elders in the desert prayed
by letting the mind sink down
into the cave of the heart

not a pail down a well
a fish flashing
home in the sea.

Home Remedy for Writer's Block

Songless, enter the forest.
Sit by the still pond
and watch the day pass
across its face.

A silver bubble
dances up from the murk,
opens its brief eye
and joins the sky.

Widening ripples
say something perfect
to something perfect
in you,

while you await
the homing of your bird.

Soundings

Not a thing
not a place
on the map of the body.

It asks for nothing
but loves when I stop
to try to feel it.

Expecting nothing
but taking more joy
in my joy than I do.

It comes in disguise—
the longing within my longing,
the place we meet.

It knows me more
than I can stand
and smiles at who I think I am.

And offers, for all the hooks
that find tender flesh,
a blanket of forgiveness.

It saves me
from the blade I wield
against myself.

It bears the unbearable
glimpse of all
that cannot stay.

Where does it hurt?
It wants to know.
How bad?

Taking the cup
of my sorrows, it drinks
and hands it back empty.

Wood Island Light

Light has a way
of playing over water

when the sun is gone
and the sea and air

turn slate and gather around you—
when the old lighthouse

on Wood Island burns
closer, like a strange new star

sending a thread of light
right to your eyes,

a thread that follows you as you walk—
invisible to others.

We each have our own, among
all the light hidden on the sea.

Vesper Lamp

If I were dying this afternoon
I would let this sheet of paper

blow away, and fling my favorite
fountain pen into the tossing grass.

The little lamp of knowing
that smoldered in these bones,

dimmed and smoky from neglect,
made visible the rooms of the world.

It never went out; it lit the space
inside the smallest things

that says *I love you.*

For God So Loved

For God so loved that
one day God wandered
the cloud of infinite love

love without end,
love without beginning
and love felt less than love.

And in that moment
before time, love knew that love
to be love, at last,

must be lost, must be given
and given until
every trace is gone.

And so God became
fire and ash and cooled into
the garden that bloomed

and crawled and stood
and walked and felt the emptiness
in the nave of the heart

where a grain of salt
from a vanished sea burns with
endless yearning.

Love becomes love
as God bleeds out all Godness
into these failing

and breakable hearts,
fleshed and tethered to hours
that dwindle towards grief.

For God so loved, God
is born and broken in each
begotten daughter's,

son's, and sparrow's fall,
a blind light that feels where
every nail has been.

Prayer of Unnaming

Let your yearning seep
into the cracks of your thoughts
about yearning.

Soak down into the place
that seems to feel and glimpse
what you truly are

which is of dust
and not dust, which is of light
and not light

where fear's edges
begin to round and melt
where desire's mirage

ceases its insatiable
gnawing inside the walls
of the small house of yourself.

Let the radiance
within the dark fill the space
where you think you live.

Your true address
is here and not here, and you
are too great and too small

to find on any map.
Your shape is the night.
You are the smooth stone,

the palm it rests in
and the ocean sculpting
it to perfect imperfection

with only the waves
and the grit of stones
washing stone away.

Rest in stillness
and feel the silence
feeling you.

The Ache

There are no experts in prayer,
only people who have been faithful to the ache.
—Macrina Wiederkehr

Even before my grandmother
drowned herself, I was lost

every plane crash,
every crippled child, every
disease without a cure.

Sometimes I still looked for Jesus
at First Baptist—Reverend Kirkland
honing in with the altar call,
to surrender, surrender all
Won't you come…
won't you come?
The choir softly quavering,
humming verse after verse—

Just as I am, without one plea
But that Thy blood was shed for me
And that Thou bid'st me come to Thee
Oh, Lamb of God, I come, I come…

The guilt and shame welled up
until I would never be loved,
unless I released my grip on the pew
and took that tearful walk
down the carpet to the foot
of the baptismal pool
to join the fold

washed in the blood.

But it didn't wash away
the daily damage
and the nightly news
from Viet Nam.

Something pulled
from the inside out.

Pulled me from my bedroom window
from the Woodstock posters
and black light mandalas
to search for a version
of myself to pull free
from the heavy syrup
of small-town Southerness.

Beyond subdivision streets,
across the state road
vacant plots were wild enough
to hide me in the weeds.

Staring into the stars,
the stillness, I vanish.

The earth is loose.
And I am home.

Walking empty beaches at the world's edge,
I turn my back to the lights of the cottages and streets,
lost in the rhythm of the swells—

drawn out of my thought-narrowed walls
to feel the pulse of my true body
before human gravity turns me back.

⁕

Sitting in a Zen meditation hall,
in the fragrance of smoldering pine—
stillness buoyed on the waves
of an ancient bronze gong,
slowing the churning of my mind
until this trance of self
dissolves in the pre-dawn stillness
of an October Saturday morning
into the waves of tires
on a wet Manhattan Street.

⁕

Kneeling in a dim cathedral,
banked with guttering votives,
a sparrow chirps in the vault
of the carved stone forest.
Every footstep, cough,
whisper merges
into the echoes of our prayer.
Pale wafers of your flesh
wait with us in the darkness.

And in silence—
my only faith.

Give it to the Flame

That almost unbearable
clarity of September
when the changing air

blows away the scrim
of summer's heat dreams
bringing us back to where we are.

Here in the parking
lot between the farmers' tents
in an old kitchen chair

a toothless minstrel
blazing with prophecy cries out
Today I am jubilant! Jubilant!

And now I must take this harvest
of straw roped to my back
and give it to the flame.

Acknowledgments

To my parents Doris and Charlie Walker, who loved and supported me, no matter where I wandered. With gratitude to my sister, Martha Walker Fullington, who's always there for me. To my special niece Katie Fullington Taylor, and all my loving family, here and in Germany.

To my mentors—J. Grady Locklear who rescued me at Sumter High School, made me poetry editor of the literary magazine, guided me towards college as an English major, and was a lifelong friend. To teacher Dwight Johnson who embodied the life of an artist and led me to opening that door. To Dr. Vincent E. Miller at Wofford College who taught me to read, write, and think in depth about literature. He took me under his wing, introduced me to tea, and opened my mind in so many ways. To poet Edward Minus who befriended me and nurtured me and my poetry. To poet Ellis Settle who valued what I was trying to say and encouraged me to keep saying it. To Mary Farkas and author Peter Haskell at the First Zen Institute in New York for years of patient support. To Philip Stephens and William Dietrich at Shalem Institute for Spiritual Guidance, who do just that, with such depth and humor.

To my writer friends—Parker Blaney, the best friend who's always sharing insights and prodding me onward and has had to read everything. To my old poetry group: Nancy and Jonathan Aldrich, Chris Queally and Alicia Fisher, for years of encouragement. To artist friends Lizz Sinclair, Robert McKibben and his beloved Susan Winn who've encouraged me so much. To Esther Cohen whose generous friendship for over forty years and invitations to join writing groups got me writing again and led to this book. To poets Beneth Sauer, Lisa Lutwyche and Pete Follansbee for ongoing inspiration. To writer and director Beaty Reynolds, and to poet Amanda Monath who felt what I meant, for their thoughtful and careful readings and major contributions to a number of my poems. To novelist Christopher Bram, friend and inspiration since our days at Scribner Book Store. To poet Philip Terman for many hours of careful editing, invaluable insights, encouragement to take risks, and an infectious love of poetry—you helped me find my voice.

With deep gratitude to Ruth Thompson and Don Mitchell for believing in me and making this book happen and for making it better with perfect suggestions. To Dr. Christian Thomas for your compassionate care.

And always to Edite Kroll, my wife and partner, whose life is writers and artists and whose passion for making things better—yes, you edited my first love poem—hopefully rubbed off on me.

Thanks to Steve Luttrell, founding editor of *The Café Review* for publishing an early version of "Girl at the Clinic." And thanks for the music, Joni Mitchell—*For the Roses* and Van Morrison—*Veedon Fleece*.

About the Author

Keith Walker grew up in North Carolina, Virginia, Tennessee and South Carolina, where he majored in English at Wofford College. In New York City, he graduated from NYU in clinical social work and has been a therapist for many years. Now in Maine for 35 years, he still eats grits for breakfast. He's been a studio potter, co-founded the Portland Zen Meditation Center in 1994, and completed the Spiritual Guidance program at Shalem Institute in Washington, DC. A handful of poets and poems have changed Keith's life, and poetry is the best way he's found to explore his experience of being and share it with others.

Printed in the USA
CPSIA information can be obtained
at www.ICGtesting.com
CBHW031902130524
8488CB00007B/102